CW00858898

Distant Ramblings

(*Poems of Life*)

By Andrew D Siddle

Contents

List of Poems

Introduction

Distant Ramblings is a collection of what I
thought to be the best of my poems since 1983.
It has taken me over thirty years to get around
to putting this little poetry book together
because life is busy and time passes so quickly.
I had great fun putting it together and I hope
you have as much fun reading it.

The Inner Self

The Inner Self

This is my oldest poem and it was written back in 1983 at a time when there was much turmoil going on in my life. I felt that I wasn't being given full ability to make my own decisions in life and this poem is a teenage attempt to describe disillusionment. Also a teenage wish to "get on" with life by making one's own decisions independently of others. The "inner self" is the real "you", or soul, hidden deep inside. The "inner self" is the actual person struggling to get out and during the years of teenage angst this is more important than at any other stage in a lifetime.

The Inner Self

For who can tell what they can see,
through veils of smoked glass melancholy,
and who can know what they believe,
when all we see we can't perceive.

When night is light,
and light is night,
and all fades out without a sight.

Through time we weave transparent lies,
and look for hope through glazed white skies,
though times may change we will not see,
with stubborn hearts that will not grieve,
for all that was and is yet to be,
will not heed my lonely plea.

To hear the wind high in the trees,
spirits soaring with the breeze,
sun baked corn breathes the name,
and all in all remains the same;
but in our hearts and minds we find,
our inner selves of distant times.

Dance of the Winter Spirits

Dance of the Winter Spirits

When the snow and ice come in winter we either love it or hate it. Dance of the winter spirits is all about blaming those good old imaginary spirits of the seasons upon every single snow flake and howling winter wind. What if that whirl wind of snow was caused by a winter Whirling Dervish outside of one's patio door? What if the large fall of snow from the front of the house was really Jack Frost jumping down from one's roof with a loud thump on to the drive?

Dance of the Winter Spirits

The crystal flakes of every morn,
that darkened husk of snow lined bower,
reveal to us the crystal power,
and the frozen gates to every dawn.

The frozen gates with frosted glaze,
which bites the flesh as to amaze,
and frosted breath at which we gaze,
whilst out-about in snowy haze.

The spirits of the crystal dawn,
dance through icy crystals born,
of this new morn lacking sun,
and onto who knows where forlorn.

For now we see Yule's frozen height,
and shivering stems give up the fight,
perhaps to rest and then anew,
then spring's new praise of new born might.

Whistling The Wind / January Tale

Whistling the Wind / January Tale

"Whistling the wind" is all about the ancient rural culture belief that if one whistles for long enough then the spirits of nature will copy. Following this the whistling howling wind will start to raise in answer to one's whistle. In the middle of winter this is combined with mornings so frozen that the frost "could take your nail". This is an old English expression to describe the pangs of pain , within the fingers, of an exceptionally freezing winter morning.

Whistling the Wind / January Tale

Perhaps one day this cold stark wind will take my
nail,
perhaps one day this wind tossed sky will surely fail,
for what darkness makes my spirit meet it's kin?
and in oh so darkened skies doth lie sin?

The feel of wind blown branches carries souls,
convincing us to stay but in our homes,
as dead and broken bracken flies the air,
and in our now warm homes why should we care?

Now branches roar and sway right to the bow,
and darkened skies still scream the mighty howl,
maybe now we feel true born nature's might,
as new year's spirit hides the old from sight.

A Small Child's Memory

A Small Child's Memory

I remember a long time ago sitting in bed because I was ill and couldn't go to school on that day. I would be about 6 or 7 years old at the time. I sat , with a hot water bottle, looking through the bedroom window at a number of oak trees way over on the horizon. My mother came up to see how I was at around midday and I just said " I want to be there mum!" "I want to be where those trees are all the way over there". I'll never forget the feeling at the time because I just wanted to be free and living with the wild trees and animals. That is the only thing that I could think of as I sat in bed, ill , staring at the mighty oak trees in the distance.

A Small Child's Memory

When I sit and watch the clouds rolling by,
sometimes I see a small child's memory,
of how the trees used to sway with the wind,
a wind that sometimes sounds like a rolling tide.

A small child's memory of awe at the sky,
that seemed somehow so big and far away,
the sun and clouds and a small child's memory,
that was mine.

So why is it that as the years flow by,
just as the tide ebbs and flows,
so the sky no longer seems big,
or far away?

Sometimes I see a small child's memory,
of how the trees used to sway with the wind,
a wind that sometimes sounds like a rolling tide,
and a memory that is mine.

The Sands of Winter

The Sands of winter

Who hasn't sat and watched the news, on television, and seen images in winter of sea spray being tossed up onto a seaside promenade. The difference between summer and winter at a seaside resort is always something that astounds me.

The Sands of Winter

The grey sky scowls at a strangely desolate sandy oasis. Not some far away desert oasis but the holiday idyll out of it's season and time. An oasis normally   dedicated to ice cream lemon tops, sunday sodas, and smoky sizzling smells and sounds. The famous oasis of plastic buckets, castles in the sand, little lords of the castle, and seaside pebble stubbed toes well out of the reach and sight of mum.

No today is different! Today the salt spray blasts instead of sprays. Rain splattered iron handrails blasted with salt spray combine with the smell of ozone, and of seaweed, against a backdrop of now tightly fastened and bolted windows. Today airborne sand fiercely blows back against the coastal road causing cars to sway and swerve against strength of wind and rain.

An occasional dog walker makes for a sad lonely shadow gripping fervently to a coated hood . Fighting forward, one step at a time, whilst the roaring wind drags every single forward foot step back again to where it came from. The sands of winter roar their delight making fun of their captive audience with bellowing haughty laughter on high. Making fun of the people who thought they had harnessed nature's cruel tide in summer. Only to be defeated by the pointing finger,of the spirit of winter, now that summer is a distant fleeting memory.

Morning Bright

Morning Bright

A poem of early morning sunrises , yawns, and a new day. A new day is a new beginning and just as a new year is a new start so can a new day be. Those few hours between day break and settling in at work determine one's mood for the rest of the entire day. Therefore each new day should be celebrated because each morning starts a whole new opportunity in life. It can be a conscious decision as to what mood one has for the rest of the day and it is therefore important to start each new day with the right frame of mind.

Morning Bright

Morning bright & another day,
chasing drowsy sleep away,
smells of coffee fill the air,
for another day to share.

Wondering what the day will bring,
plans to cherish,tunes to sing,
watching bustling people pass,
eating toast now, break that fast.

Flowers swaying as you pass,
Frantic bush birds peck the grass,
even bees they get the grasp,
of all that's planned this day to last,
now wild Vulgaris starts to dance.

Morning bright,another day,
chasing drowsy sleep away,
smells of coffee fill the air,
for another day to share.

Night Stars

Night Stars

At the age of nine I spent holiday time in Spain. I used to sit drinking chocolate milkshake and playing pinball in a modern Spanish bar at night time.
One evening I was introduced to a retired Royal Air Force officer who new about air navigation. I was absolutely fascinated by the whole thing especially about navigating an aeroplane by the stars. Anyway he and his wife took me outside in order to show me how to work out where the Pole Star and the Plough are. I didn't know anything about stars, and still don't, but even now I can remember where to find the North Star (Pole Star) and where the Plough is.

Night Stars

As I peer out through the blackened veil,
this night time cloth of light travails,
and who am I to see at all?
and what are stars that seem so small?

Cloudy wrestling swirling by,
sparkling diamonds far too high,
whirling clouds that hide the sky,
whilst cosmic ray beams try to spy.

Diamonds of the solar crown,
godly orbs that do not frown,
upon our small and mortal town,
whilst hiding under eiderdowns.

So what are these and who is there?
and why at night time do we stare?
at cosmic stars that will not share,
the solar truth; they would not dare!

Song of Mary / Dead Soul of Albion

Song of Mary / Dead Soul of Albion

This was a bit of silliness on my part. I was challenged to produce a poem, and a little tale, in four lines only. Like it or leave it there it is! A four line poem.

Song of Mary / Dead soul of Albion

She walks with a stick to the end of the crick,

many a sound from the heather she's heard,

many a song from the lowliest bird,

then skips o'er barley like some Far Tribe hick.

The Mystery Darkness

The Mystery Darkness

This is a prose poem piece which was inspired by my life whilst in West Ham in East London. I always used to enjoy walking home from the pub on an evening on my own in the dark. The reason is that I enjoy looking up at the night sky and the stars whilst I walk along. Anyway the poem's mention of burn't out cars, graffiti, and dark alleyways were all part of the kind of route that I used to use to get home to Teasal Way. Part of the poem is inspired by the Ouflow Walk close to the Abbey Mills Pumping Station in East London. Everybody in West Ham, without exception, knows where that is.

The Mystery Darkness

Once, long ago, a night drew in too quickly. In that moment, under the orange glare of street lit alleyways, I felt the darkness not only outside but somehow inside my soul as well.

Memories of darkened silhouettes against the skyline. The old pump house ugly in it's mechanical splendour. Even more so as a featured grotesque against the darkening star lined canvas of the night.

Strange thoughts that darkness is dazzling and that maybe silence is actually a kind of noise. Graffiti, barbed wire, high wire fences, burn't out cars and unseen footsteps somewhere in the distance; somewhere beyond in the midst of blackness.

All these things are a memory. The sound of water in the distance. A tide drained trickle eddying and shifting silt till tidal reverse. The stars so bright they burn and the beauty of the contemplation of solitude, almost meditation, as darkness wraps the winding black alleyways under it's unforgiving cloak.

The River

The River

Like many people I have always been very excited by waterfalls and fast flowing water. There seems to be something almost hypnotic about watching water flow be it the sea or an inland river.

The River

Gargling, bustling, roaring by,
like some bullying beast on high,
aqua blue and deepest depths,
bubbling rhythm danced in step.

Swirling white and darkest blue,
bringing dreams and memories through,
like some timeless mirror of thought,
once you look; forever caught.

With pools of dreams eddying by,
in the depths of minds eye,
images form then fade away,
like cosmic whirl pools in the fray.

Whirlpools gurgle, eddies froth,
in the depths small shadows toss,
for oh the pull of current cries,
like some giant of upper tide.

The "Other World" of Hunter's Wood

The "Other World" of Hunter's Wood

This poem was inspired by my work in Northants County, UK, In 1990/1991 I was working as a country park development officer for the creation of what were, at the time, two new countryside parks in Northamptonshire. One was the Brampton Valley Way and the other was Brixworth Country Park. The Brampton Valley Way involved rather a lot of work including laying a 14 mile granite chipping path (Granite dust laid over hardcore and lighter mixed granite aggregate), woodland management and clearance, and fencing. I have happy memories of large groups of volunteers coming over to help create woodland embankment paths, rustic steps, stiles, and woodland clearance including coppicing. I especially remember the fire that we always provided to sit around having done the work.

The Otherworld of Hunter's Wood.

The silver creamy moonlight slices through tree openings like a fine cheese knife. An opening glade lit like a searchlight from on high. Three ragged figures sit huddled around the crackling flames of a newly lit fire. Flames and smoke mingle, crackle, and cough their way around swirlingly. Billy can boiling coffee smells waft higher and higher and away over the tree canvass.

Broken over shotguns perch precariously against recently coppiced woodland stools. Gut knives glint against the growing strength of flame and stench of smoke.

No words are spoken but peacocks scream their final evening delight in the far distance. Celebrating the death of daylight as failing light now descends into the deep darkened blue of the otherworld. An Owl wafts it's wings with annoyance and swoops low enough to witness the three silent silhouettes and the crackling of flame. Bracken breaks and snaps noisily near to the surreal darkening treescape. Who is there? What is there? Who knows?

The gargling of a distant stream seems to accentuate by the mere act of transition from twilight into darkness. Finally darkness transcends the twilight world and small creatures disappear into the newly born otherworld of Hunter's wood.

A New Year

A New Year

A new year and a new start! How many times have we heard that? With new year's resolutions that we promise to keep as we break into the wonder of a new year? Well we have had the new year's celebrations so let us now see how many promises for the new year fall down into the gutter like leaves falling from an autumnal tree.Have a great year everybody.

A New Year

A new year and a new start,
that's what they say so lighten your heart,
with the old year gone there's nothing but new,
so why on earth should you still feel blue?

The turkey's gone,
and the New Year's ale,
Christmas's deceased,
New Year's pale.

So what's the new year's resolution?
To get your trusted absolution,
have we finished the New Year's vacation?,
oh forget it;   crack open another libation!.

A new year and a new start,
lift the weight up off your heart,
with new year's plans you must now dart,
if they don't work out you'll be on the cart.

The Rose

The Rose

I am a keen gardener and the rose is something that has become part and parcel of British culture despite the fact that many species originate from warmer climates elsewhere in the world. There is something very satisfying about finally seeing a rose bud appear ,and then turn into a flower, having put so much work into it's cultivation.

The Rose

Rose of old and rose of new,
you hold your head so proud and true,
with petals pure and radiant face,
your gentleness is pride of place.

Rose of old and rose of new,
through the ages so many tales have you,
is it true you once heard Vortigern's horse?
Or witnessed Offa faring the course.

Rose of old and rose of new,
yellow,white,pink or red so true,
Rose Nahema or Rose Areasia,
but your thorns bring danger to a stranger.

Rose of old and rose of new,
blood of thorn and petals new,
blossoming for all who seek delight,
for now you've reached pure beauty's height.

Celtic Dawn

Celtic Dawn

The word Celtic is one that was really invented, only a few hundred years ago, in the west.

It was invented to describe a hotch potch variety of indigenous racial groups who can all loosely be called Indo-European.Before the use of the word Celtic "Keltic" indicated a type of rural plough. Also "Keltoi" is a word in the Greek language that indicates "the hidden ones" which is it's definition. The richness of early Celtic art is amazing as was the strength of unity between people from various parts of the world united through the strength & commonality of art, spoken poetry, and culture only. In the oldest religion on the planet the Brahmanistic interpretation of God is Creator, preserver, and destroyer. By the time we reach Christianity this still exists but has been renamed as Father , Son, and Holy Spirit. Celtic culture , with it's pantheon of localised heroes and often pre Christian Saints, slots neatly between the two periods of time.

Celtic Dawn

To God in the three faces,
this morning I give you praise,
father son and spirit,
in the valley and fields of maize.

In every wild and wonderous creature,
looking to the sky,
in every morning household say,
thanks for all that's mine.

Creator, preserver,and destroyer,
all three are my Lord,
father, son, and spirit,
unto the many hordes.

Thanks for all I see today,
and thanks for all to come,
praise be as the children play,
below the morning sun.

All Hail the "Postie"

All Hail the "Postie"

I am a great fan of Royal Mail deliveries and have shown this appreciation by undertaking Royal Mail Christmas Post, and parcel sorting, at Christmas for three years in a row previously as a paid volunteer.

When one actually considers the importance of efficient logistics it becomes apparent that in terms of real worth it would be more beneficial to sing "hail" to the local postman, or postwoman, rather than a Prime Minister. Who is really more important in real terms? The world would cease to operate without efficient post, parcel, and data delivery.

That is what this poem is about.

All Hail the "Postie"

Let us now cheer with morning praise,
to the postie working all the days,
stacked up letters in a bunch,
for who knows what he hasn't a hunch!

To all the rain sodden soggy morns,
delivering letters his only cause,
and if you miss a parcel 'cause you're out to lunch,
does he moan you down or throw a punch?

No not our postie who we all praise,
out there working in the early haze,
early days and parcels due,
and we don't even have to queue.

So raise a glass for the bright red van,
and to the foot slog of this loyal man,
clattering letter boxes all the way,
you know he'll be round most every day.

Limerick of Crewe

Limerick of Crewe

A Limerick is a type of poem invented in Ireland at a place , funnily enough, called Limerick.Many contests are held to write the best Limerick , as a competition, and the Irish are correctly proud of this tradition. I wrote this limerick because I was challenged to write one so I did. Because I am not Irish I had to define it as a British Limerick. This I did by calling it Limerick of Crewe.

The rules for writing a Limerick are as follows:

- They are five lines long.
- Lines 1, 2, and 5 rhyme with one another.
- Lines 3 and 4 rhyme with each other.
- They have a distinctive rhythm.
- They are usually funny.

Limerick of Crewe

There was a young man from Crewe,

who knew not what he should do,

he decided to "fiddle" a ferry to France,

by stealing the ticket and "loot" in advance,

but ended up in Peru.

<u>Breakfast</u>

Breakfast

Breakfast and what a tradition!

It doesn't matter whether it is French style fresh hot Croissant , butter, jam and hot coffee or a more traditional full English! Just feel those taste buds going crazy for the most important meal of the day!

Bacon, baked beans, fried bread, fried eggs, saute potatoes, fried sausage, fried mushrooms and fried tomatoes. Then off out into the cold on a frosty winter morning with a warm sensation in the "tum"!

Yum!

Breakfast

Breakfast time and another day,
not letting drowsy dreamland stay.

Weetabix,
or eggs to munch,
no milk left?
Oh..... what a crunch!

Bacon, sausage and fried bread,
tomatoes & mushrooms to feed my head.

Where's the coffee?
I've smashed a cup,
the bacon's burn't,
I'm out of luck.

What's the use? I'll go back to bed,
Sort it out later! Just a sleepy head.

The Spirit of the Clouds

The Spirit of the Clouds

Hands up how many of you have ever laid down on a scorching hot grass embankment , in the middle of summer, and stared at the sky? I certainly have! It is a British cultural pastime to stare at the summer sky, at the clouds roaming by, and imagine their shape to be something else other than that which it is.

The Spirit of the Clouds

Splash of white,
you're canvassed well,
on azure secrets,
none can tell.

Who hides behind your silken flight?
what creature knows your course till night?
With feathered fingers grasping well,
and shapes that form from unchaste light.

That spirit hides we know for sure,
in every cloud of haute couture,
what sees it from it's canvas blue?
What mean we to it; and it to you?

But now I'll tell a tale so true,
it travels round the aqua blue,
with grinning face gliding by,
the spirit of the clouds flies high.

The Big Deal

The Big Deal

Some people dream of getting that final "big deal" in life. Maybe the one final big deal that they will retire upon and never need to work again. Others, such as myself, like work and wouldn't really know what to do without our usual profession, or trade, to keep our minds occupied for life.

This is a poem for all those seeking to make it big this year with that final "big one"!

The Big Deal

Get that deal for it's a steal,
when they come a' running don't even feel,
cash in the pocket and hi fly dreams,
just sign on the dotted line & I'll be full of beams.

Hey mister that's my cash,
just phone the centre they've got a stash,
you mean more to a donkey than a bucket of eels,
I mean that most sincerely folks now turn on your
heels.

See the rain fall to the sound of crashing change,
it comes in red or blue but I can always re-arrange,
if you want I can change it just give me a bell,
but don't open the wrapper or I can't re-sell.

Cheque or credit we charge 12%,
and if you buy now you'll see it's heaven sent,
just open your wallet show the colour of your cash,
right that's deal done sorry I've got to dash!

Docked in Port

Docked in Port

One of my ascendants was Captain Robert Newman of the British merchant navy back in the 1800's. Captain Newman was the skipper of the Tiberius that sailed out of New York Harbour, USA, in the late 1800's only to vanish without a trace. It never reached the United Kingdom.

It is tales such as this that leave me with a sense of wonder about the sea and about the people who work on it. This sense of wonder inspired the following poem.

Seafaring terms are used as a metaphor for the physical acts of love, in a relationship, in a way that is not supposed to be too serious.

Docked in Port

I sailed my ship so long and so far,
with binoculars to read from the stars,
but none could I see with arms held wide,
till your love port did I gladly glide.

My sails I flew high and billowing out,
I climbed the ladder solid and proud,
hoisting my main sail so firmly be,
till in sight of land you called on to me.

Offloading the treasures from my inner most hold,
I beckoned you closer for me to be bold,
of all the true things held dearly within,
now I know the feeling is not just a whim.

With my cargo unloaded I held you so close,
your long blowing hair I cherished the most,
with horizons a'new from a sea shanty scene,
I now keep your image so open and seen.

Hoisting my flag I now surely pull out,
out from your love port but there's hardly a doubt,
though I sail far and wide I'll hold you so dear,
and when close to your love port it'll always be clear.

<u>She</u>

<u>She</u>

This is a little poem I did in appreciation of the female form. Namely the one that I am with but it could just as well be any woman anywhere in the world.

I called the poem simply she. This is because perfection does not require anything other than a simple word to describe it. So here it is...........She:

She

If curves that swerve,
where all like yours,
I'd tell the rest,
they're nought but bores.

That deepest button of belly so set,
caressed by hand and hugged with zest.
darkest hair that blows like reeds,
spread around to all my needs.

Your sparkling eyes that mirror your thoughts,
deep set coals that capture my sort,
the sway of an angel from side to side,
that flick of your hair that builds delight.

Legs so brown,
they need to be seen,
and all those curves,
that leave me so keen.

Coffee Time

Coffee Time

Here is a tribute to the coffee bean. A tribute to all of those hours I have worked, sitting at a desk , sometimes only kept awake by that vital mug of dark brown boiling bean. For all coffee lovers this poem is a must.

Coffee Time

Sit and relax the day can wait,
time for coffee? It's a date!,
fresh and strong it's smell to be,
strong and fresh just as you see.

Deep and dark it's depths you'll find,
in coffee cup, or the mug behind,
smells waft from an open door,
roasted wonders like never before.

Cafeine spikes your tired mind,
taking you away from the long days grind,
just one cup and you will see,
coffee!; "it's the drink for me!".

One more cup and then on with work,
relax and drink without a slurp,
drink your coffee and share with me,
all the wonders of the coffee bean.

Midday

Midday

Midday and what an odd time to be. Not the start and not the finish just something in between mid way. Not quite lunch time and well beyond breakfast time. So midday is when we maybe go to get a quick snack to be eaten whilst working. It is maybe when we think about what we have achieved during the morning. It is maybe when we think about what we still have to achieve during the rest of the day.

Midday

Midday and all's O.K.,
half way through the working day,
neither morn' nor time to go,
your mornings efforts will surely show!

Telephone calls and conference meets,
out to dinner and there we'll seat,
frantic problems settled fast,
business suits and polished glass.

Mobile phones and satellite maps,
pound the streets and check your 'apps',
Ipad dreams and polished shoes,
never too late to check the news!

Clouds roll by from a 9th floor seat,
now go to reception meet and greet,
files piled high in work to do,
time for a snack chockie I choose.

Pie n' a Pint

Pie n' a Pint

The great London culture tradition of "pie n' a pint" is one that is unlikely to die. Pie n' a pint; that traditional delicacy of the London boroughs palate. Pie n' a pint that tourists come in their hordes to sample in their own right.

Pie n' a pint. Brought all the way down through history books from the ancient traditions of the "**Pien'** " dynasty maybe?

Pie n' a pint Guv' and leave the rest to me! Nod is as good as a wink to a blind man in the cellar! Know what I mean John?

Here is the poem : Pie n' a pint!

Pie n' a Pint

When all the days work is finished and done,
there's just one thing that carries me on,
pie n' a pint and your very best ale,
pie n' a pint and I'll tell you a tale.

In ancient Egypt they started to fight,
when the hops were stolen one cloudless night,
Beershimi tribe thieves stole Pharaoh's best brew,
of the old 'beer worship' that's oh so true!.

Now in ancient Rome they may have drunk wine,
but Boudicca drank beer all of the time,
so when Ceasar fermented the luscious red grape,
Iceni resolved to lick him into shape.

Now whilst it's true that the Vikings drank mead,
Wessex were shocked; it's against our creed!
We only want beer; so the Vikings went to war,
the whole lot were slaughtered and never seen no
more.

When all the days work is finished and done,
there's just one thing that carries me on,
pie n' a pint and your very best ale,
pie n' a pint and I'll tell you a tale.

Jack Hammer Blues / Burnley Overture

Jack Hammer Blues / Burnley Overture

This poem was inspired by a song of the same name written by Woody Guthrie in the USA. I am a fan of blues music so it made sense to call the poem Jack Hammer Blues. I am also involved with the property and land industries, for a living, so I like the image of a Jack Hammer in use for the poem. The "Burnley Overture" part arises because I was born in Padiham, Lancashire, where I lived for the first three years of my life before moving south. The poem is therefore written in the localised Lancashire way of speaking.

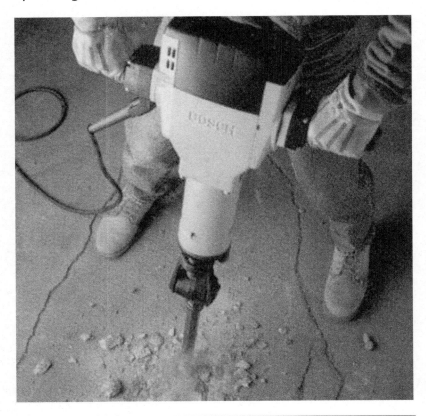

Jack Hammer Blues / (Burnley Overture)

T' proudest day in all 'o me life,
were when I were bought t' Jack Hammer by me wife,
now you may well say that's a funny thing to do,
but she knew what I like and 'er love for me were true.

Hammering 'ere and 'ammering there,
I got to be known most everywhere,
I've n'er felt so proud and tall,
bouncin' up and down it t'were a real right ball.

Oh you ought t' 'ave seen the smile on me face,
with a Jack Hammer wobble all o'er the place,
now I know you'll say it surely aint true,
but without me 'ammer there'd be nothin' else to do.

The day me wife died and ascended from this place,
I jack 'ammered round 'er grave and knocked it into shape,
now the people just stared at such a mad thing to do,
but that's mad ' ammer John and the Jack Hammer blues.

Struttin' with Attitude / Anorak Stroll

Struttin' with Attitude / Anorak Stroll

Like many people I have had a love of both Reggae and
Rastafarian culture since being introduced to it by the song
"Dreadlock Holiday" written by 10CC in the 1970's. This poem is
about an ordinary British chap , on his way to the local library,
who meets a Rastafarian standing in a doorway.

Struttin' with Attitude / Anorak Stroll

Walking down Johnson Street one day,
headed for my daily municipal library stay,
I was making good time walking on my own,
I knew by 5 I'd be on my way home.

As I walked down by the railway archway store,
well I didn't even notice how the air was raw,
all of a sudden a dark voice behind suddenly said:-

"strut it cool!"

I said you what?

"Chill....strut it cool!"

Well I felt like a clot!

I couldn't figure out what the guy was on about,
so at the library I got a book; nice an' stout,
"strutting on by with a chill in the eye",
well I knew what I wanted and I felt really high.

The book said:-

>To strut with a chill,
>You 'as to 'ave the will,
>let it all hang out,
>so there'll be no doubt,
>hold your shoulders right back,
>or you'll look like a gnat,
>sway your body to your height,
>then you'll be doin' quite alright.

(continued on next page)

So I went outside and I walked down the street,
it didn't take long till I got it really neat,
the first person that I met,
I decided to accept.

I said:

"strut it cool!"

She said you what?

" Chill....strut it cool!"

she looked like a clot!

Well that's how I finished "me" day anyway.
Nice to be able to get me anorak and woolly mitts
off after all that fuss and bother!

Beans for Me

Beans for Me

Beans on toast 'eh? Who doesn't love baked beans? Well I'll tell you the truth. Up until about the age of nine I didn't like the look of baked beans at all. I refused to even try so much as one baked bean up until this age.

Then one day I finally tried my first baked bean and suddenly the whole world opened up. Yes the whole world opened up for me and I started to sing "**Beanz Meinz Heinz**" ad lib (*ad nauseam*).

Thereafter life consisted of secretly making hot buttered toast, and baked beans, every time there was nobody about at home as an extra daytime snack.

So let's hear it for the humble bean!

Beans for Me

Let me tell you all of a secret craze,
the great baked bean of modern days,
that perfect bean so small and clean,
tomato sauce sploshes as it gleams.

See happily belching bumbling bards,
eaten the lot? You've had your cards!,
Flatulence and happy grunts,
tomato stains and dropped bean hunts.

Stained shirts reddened with our old friend,
the great baked bean until the end,
fork flicked goodies bomb the floor,
the flying bean as never before!

If the greatest men of olden times,
had eaten baked beans they'd have had a gold mine,
for all the battles ever lost,
if they'd only eaten beans there'd have been no cost.

No Where to go and All that Jazz

No Where to Go and All that Jazz

This is a poem about that Thursday evening feeling. That feeling that it isn't the weekend yet but **"I really want to go someplace"**. No friends are available, boredom is rising, and what is to be done about it?

 "And all that jazz" means **"and so on and so forth"** but for those who like jazz music it also means a visit to a local jazz club in the evening.

No Where to go and All that Jazz

Thursday night and nowhere to go!
Totally bored and nothing on the radio,
tried the T.V. , seen it all before!
Nothing doing & nobody is at the door.

Where's that Kaz I'll give her a ring,
Oh, you're not coming out, 'cause it's not your sort of
thing?
Oh well there goes another one, oh what's it all for?
I want to go somewhere and they're all being a bore.

I'll peek through the blind and look over the road,
what are THEY up to? Why that slimey toad!
I'll not call around there again and that's the lot,
Well , not today anyhow, I'll take a look tomorrow at what
they've got!

Oh for a fun packed show with some jazz,
dazzle them all out with the old "razzamatazz",
but not tonight I'll just sit here and be austere,
Oh what's the point I'll crack open another beer.

Thursday night and nowhere to go!
Totally bored and nothing on the radio,
tried the T.V., seen it all before!
Nothing doing & nobody is at the door.

Morning in the Summer Lands

Morning in the Summer Lands

In Dark Age Britain, or Albion, it was normal procedure for a Royal Family, and army, to have a summer residence and a winter residence. So basically the year would be split into two segments and one would move between one home and another depending on the time of year. Indeed it would be normal, in many instances, to use a fortified castle abroad during the winter months in some cases.

The **Summerland is also** the name given by **Theosophists**, **Wiccans** and some earth-based **contemporary pagan** religions to their conceptualization of an **afterlife**. The common portrayal of the Summerland is as a place of rest for souls in between their earthly incarnations.

Morning in the Summer Lands

For what is this morning glow
that meets my tired eyes?

as awakening chattering birds
greet the morning skies

awakening our slothful rest
to the busy buzzing bees

and little brown mice that dart
through the wheat fields and the trees.

Oh glory to the summer oak
to his regal arms be peace

and hail the summer golden skies
above the babbling geese

as gargling golden springs
whisper of the time

when summer's golden spirits
drove the darkness from our eyes

I see the sun soaked corn
glow brightly in the light

as sharp cut new mown lawns
seem to whisper of the sight

of worldly wizened toads
who speak of all that's right

through all this golden haze
in summer's shimmering height.

Plaice n' Chips n' Mushy Peas

Plaice n' Chips n' Mushy Peas

At the age of thirteen years and ten months I applied for my very first job which was at a fish and chip shop in the evenings. At the age of 14 I then started work. I later went on to devise my own style of batter mix which I still use at home for frying fish.

Plaice n' Chips n' Mushy Peas

Plaice n' chips n' mushy peas,
the secret batter just to please,
served at eight and try not to be late,
got a right "belcher" 'ere so 'old out "yer" plate.

When I was young I learn't a skill,
the secret of the battered eel,
then moved on to a more luxurious fate,
battered plaice right on "yer" plate.

The batter of the "chip monk" Gods,
"fat fryers" fail it's against the odds,
to see the secret of the batter true,
just "scoff" it down 'cause I won't tell you!

Mixing, slopping, showering flour,
whilst waiting for that sacred hour,
when all come around to proudly see,
plaice n' chips n' mushy peas.

Big Bill and Gertrude – Holiday Time Again

Big Bill and Gertrude - Holiday Time Again

This is a not too serious tribute to the great British fortnightly summer holiday.

To all of those stubbed toes on the beach wearing flip flops. To all of those ice cream cones with a lemon top. To all of those arguments as to where to go first. To all of those dozy hot sleeping sessions on a sandy beach smothered with sun tan oil.

The great British holiday!

Big Bill and Gertrude - Holiday Time Again

Will you marry me Gertrude?
said big Bill in the sun one day,
Gertrude said "no"!
So he got a beer; and drank it right away.

Will you come for a swim in the sea?
said Bill to Gertrude May,
Gertrude said no!
So Bill swam on his own; around the bay.

Will you come for dinner,
in your posh frock of deepest blue?
Gertrude said "not likely!",
I'm going to the Bingo and not with you!.

So at last our happy couple,
head home from western shore,
a holiday shared most brightly,
from the heart of Rickman shore.

The Friday Night Special

The Friday Night Special

Friday night and time for the lad's night out. No work tomorrow so it's beer and more beer maybe followed by a night club when the pubs shut.

Sound familiar?

Go for it….…...it's the Friday night special!

The Friday Night Special

Friday night & the end of the week,
the end of work so let's take a peek,
at the wonderous social life all around our town,
Oh yep I know John; yours is Newky Brown.

Smoky pool rooms on the rave,
they all know the barman's name is Dave,
where're the ciggies, now here's the crunch,
no more change mate! What a dunce!

Line up the bevvies three by three,
I reckon that's one for you and two for me,
how much do you want guv'? No it's on the tab,
he's lost his wallet, well that's too bad.

Beer and chips and mushy peas,
hold on a minute I need a; key,
to all the night holds on the raz,
bright lights, dizzy heads, and a girl called Kaz.

Just a Face

Just a Face

Sometimes the first person in a lifetime to strike alight the vital flame of love is the one who's face never really dies in the memory. The face seems to hide somewhere in the back of one's mind and is always sitting in the subconscious, somewhere, simmering away like a gas hob burner on minimum temperature setting.

This is a prose poem about the memory of a first love.

Just a Face

Somewhere in the dimmest depths of the surreal lies my memory of a face. The first face that I ever held near, the first face that I thought true and dear, but a face that is always there in the back of my very being.

What a thing to believe that after all this flowing and eddying of time her face still hides inside me. Somewhere deep but somewhere still there. She lives and is still hiding there , somewhere, in the back of my mind. In my very being.

To see her face true all this time on? Her face inside my thoughts. Hiding under my thoughts of everyday chores. The face of the past overlays her image now with tears. Lost in memories of what should have been and what could have been but is lost.

The first one I held near to me and the one I should have held dear to me. The yesteryear face is all my soul will stand. Roll back the years and return to me the face of my innermost being. Or let me go.

Angel

Angel

There are two ways of looking at the word angel. It can be either considered as a term of endearment or as a mystical interceder between heaven and earth.

Wikipedia defines an angel as:-

one of a class of spiritual beings; a celestial attendant of God. In medieval **angelology**, angels constituted the lowest of the nine celestial orders (seraphim, cherubim, thrones, dominations or dominions,virtues, powers, principalities or princedoms, archangels, and angels).

__Angel__

If I called you angel,
would you call me silly?
for all the world is turning,
in a way that is not willing!

Not willing to remember,
the joys of souls entwined,
nor the feel of warmth from words alone,
no stranger to our kind!

A world that will not wait,
for a patient word of praise,
nor a gentle stroke of hair,
in twilight's dim lit haze.

So in what sense is it better?
to briskly walk away,
when all you need's inside you,
to find a better day.

Saturday Lie In

Saturday Lie In

It is early Saturday morning and you are sleeping off the night out on friday evening that drifted into Saturday morning. It is light but the curtains are still drawn. The person you love in life is lying next to you and thoughts of work can wait until monday.

That is what Saturday mornings are for!

Saturday Lie In

Yawn away the feather warm morn,
don't get up the day's not yet born,
warm and tucked up with feather eider,
where I can snuggly really hide here.

Open one eye, no!........ roll over and snore,
breakfast to make? Oh what a bore,
slumberland saturdays and drift away dreams,
no one to bother me or so how it seems.

Saturdays were made for such dozing,
too cold outside so keep those snug toes in,
snoring warm bliss how good can this be?
with my tired girl snuggled next to me.

Of Joe McRead

Of Joe McRead

This is a poem about a fictitious character Joe McRead. Somebody who maybe used to have his own wife and home but now sleeps rough. Somebody who sleeps on a park bench , uses cardboard and newspaper to keep warm, and has a dog to set against anybody who disturbs him in the early hours. A man who drinks cheap cider or meths if collected coins run short.

Of Joe McRead

An old park bench and scuffed laceless boots,
That'll be your bed if you aint got no roots,
old Joe McRead and his one eyed dog,
living for the day when he's going to stay with God.

Meths and apples from the supermarket skip,
a sandwich, or two, discarded by a school trip,
newspapers under coat to keep toastie and warm,
and a couple of bin liners 'cause there's going to be a storm.

So who knows Joe and where he's been?
Did he once have a home or always a "lonester" is he seen,
old Joe carries a knife glinting nice and sharp,
and if you get his back up you'd better start to dart.

Some say Joe knows every skip in town,
and out in the sun all day he's always a shade of brown,
but all that Meths and cider in his head,
just don't talk when you pass 'cause he's like the living dead.

So there's old Joe McRead and his one eyed dog,
the mid morning sun brings a lifting of the fog,
carefully packing belongings, bin liners, and paper bags,
and off before the park warden ; he's always been a nag.

If I Say "Om" What do You Know?

If I Say "Om" What do You Know?

In this day and age, with high stress jobs and high stress performance targets in the commercial market place, relaxation is more important than ever. High blood pressure and erratic breathing are detrimental to one's health and also cloud accurate and sensible solutions within decision making.For this reason I am an advocate of meditation skills and breathing control skills.I have been since having been taught the skills in the early 1980's. This poem is about the astral plane and meditation.

If I Say 'Om' what do You Know?

If I say Om,
how would you show?
from Alpha to Omega,
what do you know?

Clear your mind,
then go with the flow,
leave your thoughts,
for the Astral show.

The Astral Plane is but a blink away,
leave your troubles; blow them away,
go for 5 minutes,
go far away.

Just clear your mind,
and free your soul,
now feel the peace,
away you go.

If I say Om,
how would you show?,
from Alpha to Omega,
what do you know?

I'd Scupper for a "Cuppa"

I'd Scupper for a "Cuppa"

Be it Earl Grey or just a Typhoo brew up from a tea bag the mid morning "cup of char" is a great tradition to be upheld as British culture. Tea first became established in Britain because of the influence of a foreign princess, **Catherine of Braganza**, the queen of Charles II. A lover of tea since her childhood in Portugal, she brought tea-drinking to the English royal court, and set a trend for the beverage among the aristocracy of England in the seventeenth century.

I'd Scupper for a "Cuppa"

Now tendrils of winter's smite abound,
there's one thing in mind that I'm allowed,
to offset the feel of frost that's around,
that's a cup of tea boiling hot and "sound".

Born of India's fragrant flight,
aromatic scent of exotica in sight,
dark and knowing depths you'll see,
in our own cup of "Rosie Lee".

From Earl Grey to Typhoo's own,
without a cuppa they'll surely moan,
for what man in his right mind said,
we're out of tea ! Are you out of your head?

What could beat that sensual feel,
with tea drunk we're men of steel,
good for morning, noon, or night,
don't give it up 'cause "it'll see you right".

The old tea pot it tells a tale,
of three generations of tea that we hail,
as the staunch bench mark of a cultural trait,
'cause if you aint got tea you're the one that they'll
hate!

Omar Khayyam the Stitcher of Time

Omar Khayyam the Stitcher of Time

Omar Khayyam is one of my favourite poets alongside maybe William Butler Yeats. I have a copy of the Rubaiyat written by Omar Khayyam and it is a book that my ascendants also new. My grandmother, Edith, on my father's family side died with a copy of the book in her hand with her thumb turning over the page of her favourite poem therein.

So here is my tribute to the life of old Omar. Omar the tent maker. Omar the Sultan's friend. Omar the astronomer. Omar the teacher. Omar the mathematician, Omar the hated, Omar the loved, Omar the philosopher. Omar the poet.

Omar Khayyam!

Omar Khayyam the Stitcher of Time

Alas poor Omar for the desert winds have gone,
and now new times and ways that will so now belong,
to all that saw truth as you had seen,
the beauty of the stars and of the teachings you were so keen.

The reddest wine no longer flows behind your private door,
nor do the pupils honour you with smallest gifts for you to store,
for all the sultan's strength and all the sultan's might,
couldn't stop old Omar's soul within the eastern winds take
flight.

Of all your tents the bedouin gave you praise,
your poems by night and your stitching by days,
of all your thoughts , and stars, and maps,
within the Rubaiyat you have left a clue perhaps.

So now as years have gone by,
we raise a glass to the soul that would not die,
old Omar has lifted the veil of life to see,
all that was, all that is, and all that is yet to be.

Thoughts of an Insomniac

Thoughts of an Insomniac

Ever had one of those nights when no matter what
you attempt to do it is just possible to get to sleep?
Tossing and turning, turn from right to left, turn
from left to right, oh where has the duvet gone?

Do you struggle to get to sleep no matter how tired
you are? Or do you wake up in the middle of the
night and lie awake for hours, anxiously watching
the clock? Insomnia is a common problem that takes
a toll on your energy, mood, health, and ability to
function during the day.

This is a prose poem for all those sleepless people
out there.

Thoughts of an Insomniac

I wonder if I shut my eyes now maybe the night glare of blackness will go! Go where though? ....and how can darkness be seen as a type of light anyway?

Where are all those sleep sheep I once heard of when young? If I count them faithfully, every single one, then surely I will awake them! If I awake them surely they will bleat and then we will all be awake and not just me.

Perhaps if I roll over this way, no maybe the other way, or better still lie on my back where I was before! Yes, where I was before the thought even came into my head.

What is the time? Oh why is the illuminated clock face so bright I will never now sleep? Perhaps I could cut the clock power and return to darkness.....but if I do I shall wonder what time it is and then I will never find restful sleep.

Trains in the distance, wind in the trees, cars passing by,......no! All now leave please! For thinking about sleeplessness is surely tiring....Perhaps if I just fetch one cup of coffee to help me think clearly? Then the night may pass me by.

Ode to Sense and Sensibility / Sense at Last!

Ode to Sense and Sensibility / Sense at Last!

I remember when I was at school one particular teacher would always say "now will you please be sensible" to the class. So I recently thought to myself "**well why not write a poem about sense and sensibility**" and put completely the opposite, to being sensible, in as the contents.

The words **Sense and Sensibility** were the title for a book written by **Jane Austen** in the year 1811 and published under her alias name "**The Lady**". My poem is rather in the style of the American writer **Edgar Alan Poe** who was born in 1809.

I like this poem and had a lot of fun writing it.

Ode to Sense and Sensibility - Sense at Last!

If terrible tidal torrents,
try your tired brain,
then track the tiny trembling Taag,
through the bushes from wherest they came.

If timid tolly toadstools,
tie you to your trellis ,
then take the tact of the Tolly cat,
and try once more again.

When trying tenacious torracks tumble,
timbling towards your door,
tremble totally nimbling fast,
and vanish through the door.

But if all is lost in Tangle Tork,
beware the tiny Taag,
who treddle through your timble town,
and talk of huggle hark.

Freedom is a Highway to the Coast

Freedom is a Highway to the Coast

I was born in the 1960's and quickly became true to the culture of my birth decade. Hippydom, freedom of the road, freedom of the soul, and the rights of the individual have always played an essential mainframe to what I believe in and who I am.

One of the easiest ways to feel a kind of freedom without affecting others too greatly is simply by free travel and exploration. This is therefore the justification for the title to this poem Freedom is a highway to the coast.

Freedom is a Highway to the Coast

What is freedom have you ever thought?
One thing or another depending on your type and sort,
freedom from bickering & freedom from strife,
freedom from rules and entrapment for life.

Is freedom anarchy or is it something else?
Freedom can be sanity but to another a personal hell,
so why the difference as to what freedom can be?
Different views are "a freedom" and that is the key.

Freedom to me is an open road,
clear sky above me and never being told,
what I should do or who I should be,
freedom is enlightment and I keep it close to me.

Some seek comfort within local rules,
and security in being governed by some who are but fools,
to those who seek freedom their opinion is not covered,
because at the end of the day it's the same as being smothered.

There's a difference between "control freak" and "rule of law",
"Law" is to be applauded the former are just a bore,
so when you see somebody who is not under control,
perhaps you didn't see; it's freedom of the soul.

Freedom was given to us by the all knowing God,
to those of us who know him it doesn't even seem odd,
so who is in charge now is it "mankind" or the "almighty force" ?
If you don't know him it's mankind; you know my answer of
course!

Which Way to the "Municipal"?

Which Way to the "Municipal"?

This is a poem for all of you travellers who are visiting a town or city that you have never been to before. A poem for people who have lost their way and can't change lane. A poem for the traffic jam from hell itself. A poem for the driver who has just been rammed by the car behind having changed lane to narrowly avoid being hit by an HGV.

Which Way to the "Municipal"?

Road signs, old signs, diversions that are new,
which way to the municipal?
I haven't got a clue!

Left or right? I'll try the middle lane,
straight out of town again,
oh what a serious pain.

Flying over fly overs; aren't you glad that you came?
road traffic diversion,
it's always been the same.

Lights that flash amber & lights that flash blue,
what a load of pretty lights,
yes, I can see too.

Arrow to the left and arrow to the right,
I love those little arrows,
they're almost out of sight.

Lorry in your lane,
well it's starting to rain,
smell that gorgeous diesel; glad that you're sane?

Where Be the Blues?

Where Be the Blues?

From J J Cale, to Cream, and on to B.B. King I have been a fan of rhythm & Blues ,and Blues, since as long as I can remember. So this is a poem dedicated to one of my favourite music styles.

Where be the blues bro'? Where be the blues?

Where Be the Blues?

Blues is a feeling you get when you're down,
play it in twelve bar & they'll give you the crown,
give me a blues scale from A to G,
when I hear the old blues I know what can be.

To be down is to be up,
to be blue is to be bright,
it may be confusing,
just say that I'm right.

From a grinding guitar to a beat box base,
blues is all clear now so say that it's ace,
from B.B. King to our old friends Cream,
let it all groove now it's just how you dreamed.

Grinding and slow or build up the beat,
add the star solo and say that it's neat,
blues is a feeling that makes some feel bad,
a deep coloured feeling that everyone has.

<u>Spirit of Envy</u>

Spirit of Envy

Envy is a terrible human emotion and one that leads to self destruction as it can cause poor health when taken to the extreme. Envy is also part of the Catholic Christian seven deadly sins. The seven deadly sins, so called, include:-

- **Lust**
- **Gluttony**
- **Greed**
- **Sloth**
- **Wrath**
- **Envy**
- **Pride**

We don't live in a perfect world so nobody is perfect. However early Christian priests tried to use these points in order to instruct as to the best way to exist as a united community.

Spirit of Envy

If I offered to share with you everything that is mine,
would you just sit and stare; accusing me of being sublime?
Heart of ice with eyes of steel,
questioning every single thing that I feel.

Why do you slate me,
when I tell a joke?
For what purpose is that look in your eye,
you'd much rather I choke.

If I gave you my world,
would you throw it away?
With swirling clouds unfurled,
spirit of envy is here to stay.

So I'll sing you a song,
of the beauty of the dawn,
and how we both knew all along,
you've felt envy since I was born.

The Sun

The Sun

Over the centuries various cultures and races have thought the Sun to be a special Godly being. Obviously if the sun creates vegetation and life, through photo synthesis, then there must be something or other to this point of view however simple it is.

Anyway this is a poem praising the sun.

The Sun

Golden fire Lord of the sky,
heroic Aten King of high,
tales of your long past abound,
all secrets kept without a sound.

Heroic fire ball flaming by,
all who challenge you fail and die,
your solar flares they burn the air,
as you travel on both true and fair.

Spitting from a fiery tongue,
but with the moon rise your work is done,
travelling through the sky by day,
but resting when the moon God plays.

Every morning when you show your face,
the moon God flees without a trace,
but we know he is hiding and shy,
then comes back again when you pass by.

Phoenix

Phoenix

Wikipedia defines the phoenix as follows:-

In **Greek mythology,**
a **phoenix** or **phenix** (**Greek**: φοῖνιξ *phoinix*) is a
long-lived **bird** that is cyclically regenerated or
reborn. Associated with the **sun**, a phoenix obtains
new life by arising from the ashes of its predecessor.

Some would say the word **"Phoenix"** was actually
used as a metaphor for an historical description of
the death and rebirth of Phoenician culture in
history. The last famous homeland of the
Phoenicians was Carthage in North Africa following a
westerly movement away from Sidon and Tyre in
classical Phoenicia itself. Also the famous Tarshish
fleet of ships that were moored in southern Spain
north of Africa.One may take the Phoenix to be a
mythical bird or a metaphor for Phoenician culture as
one wishes.

Phoenix

Oh bird of fire born of destruction,
see the burning of corruption,
as you soar from the burning dead,
now tell the future for us ahead.

Mythical bird of a long dead race,
feathers burning golden now gather pace,
leave behind all that is old and decayed,
transcend the smoke and all who stayed.

Concrete shudders glass blows out,
bricks they crumble & people shout,
flames rip flesh right to the bone,
as people find they have no home.

Of all other birds there are none as sublime,
mythical power smashes them from the sky,
the end of a city exploding with force,
the start of a new time with old Phoenix of course.

Of Time and Anti Time

Of Time and Anti Time

A poem dedicated to time. Where does it go? Does anybody know? Time speeding up & time slowing down. Time to move on & time to sit down.

Of Time & Anti Time

Time my old friend where have you gone?
You always stood by me whether I was right or wrong,
do you now smite my me straight into my face,
your cruel hearted passage leaves barely a trace.

Time comes " a' knocking " upon my front door,
ticking and a chiming as it always has before,
maybe a line on the face or stiffness of pace,
but time I defy you to keep in your place.

Was it yesterday I watched our collie bound over fields?
or was it "over thirty" since he fell down and keeled,
the time of a slow chime mocking my stance,
the ticking and the tocking like some old time dance.

Of all my deeds remembered be they good or be they bad,
but never caught out; some wish that they had,
for when all is said and done there is zero left to say,
people come and go up to our dying day.

Sunrise and sunset to a metronome sound,
moonrise and moon fall until I hit the ground,
but "oh to grasp" just one nettle of time,
and therein firmly hold it preserved in it's prime.

Where are They? / Old Time Reunion No. 501

<u>Where are They? / Old Time Reunion No. 501</u>

Some people make an awful fuss about school reunions, old tie networks, and staying in touch with long ago contacts. I have no objection to this but have a different culture.

I started my first job at fourteen years old. At the age of fifteen I was doing a forty hour week working for two firms, at weekends and in the evenings, as well as still signing in at school during the daytime. By the age of just over fifteen I had completely lost interest in school and was thinking , at the back of my mind, about what I could do to set up my own business in the future.

There is little point in talking to somebody who is street wise "educated" about old time school reunions. Such people have had to fight "tooth and nail" for everything in life. Rough diamonds , one and all, and with the street scars to prove it!

Where are They? / Old Time Reunion No. 501!

Some talk a little while of old friends gone,
some grew old, some died, some got the whole of life wrong,
and the motley crew that I once begot,
all drfited off and that was the lot.

From the sixties on to the millenium and ten,
where are they now and who was I then?
some talk of old times and take off their hat,
but I see the past's dead & that's the end of that.

Gangs of kids that crowded the streets,
I was there too and all eating sweets,
then the teenage years of beer and fights,
and oh those bright stars throughout those wild nights.

But if it's gone, then it's gone, farewell and goodbye,
in the praise of my soul mate, my growth of soul, you decry,
for as my life spark unites at once with she,
your memory now goes, adios, from me.

The Beginning and the End

The Beginning and the End

It is difficult to know what to put at the end of a little book of poetry so I wrote this one especially to finish off. It is called **The Beginning and the End**. From Alpha to Omega . Alpha (A) and **omega** (Ω) are respectively the first and last letters of the Classical (Ionic) **Greek alphabet**. This would be similar to referring to someone in English as the "A and Z".

Alpha and Omega are also mentioned in the Book of Revelation in Christianity: " It is done. I am Alpha and Omega, the beginning and the end. I will give unto him that is athirst of the fountain of the water of life freely".

On that note this little book of poems now ends.

The Beginning and the End

This is where it STARTS,
with poems from the heart,
thoughts from nowhere swirl around,
raise a fish net and bring them down.

Thoughts of words and rhyme and trends,
moods and feelings gather as old friends,
take those moods and colour with prose,
for where it comes from nobody knows.

Now this is where it ENDS,
from Alpha to Omega in emotive trends,
a poetic vision finished and stored,
raise their interest and they'll never be bored.

The end of a poem penned and typed,
the essence of being and all that is right,
within the deep side of your mind,
found in all of us of the human kind.

Acknowledgement

All of the poems in this book were written between 1983 and 2015. It would not have been possible to complete this project without the encouragement and support of Kevin, owner of the poetry portal known as Allpoetry.com, and for his help in registering copyright for these poems.

Printed in Great Britain
by Amazon

85273473R00119